Land of Liberty

Montana

by Mike Graf

Consultant:
Timothy J. LeCain, Ph.D.
Assistant Professor of History
Montana State University

Capstone press
Mankato, Minnesota

Capstone Press
151 Good Counsel Drive • P.O. Box 669 • Mankato, Minnesota 56002
http://www.capstone-press.com

Library of Congress Cataloging-in-Publication Data
Graf, Mike.
  Montana / by Mike Graf.
  p. cm.—(Land of liberty)
  Contents: About Montana—Land, climate, and wildlife—History of Montana—
Government and politics—Economy and resources—People and culture.
  ISBN 0-7368-2184-8 (hardcover)
  1. Montana—Juvenile literature. [1. Montana.] I. Title. II. Series.
F731.3.G73 2004
978.6—dc21   2003000801

Summary: An introduction to the geography, history, government, politics, economy,
resources, people, and culture of Montana, including maps, charts, and a recipe.

Editorial Credits
Amanda Doering, editor; Jennifer Schonborn, series and book designer; Enoch
    Peterson, illustrator; Heather Atkinson, photo researcher; Eric Kudalis,
    product planning editor

Photo Credits
Cover images: Mountains at Glacier National Park, North Wind Picture Archives;
    cattle and cowboys, Corbis/Brian A. Vikander

Capstone Press/Gary Sundermeyer, 54; Corbis/Charles E. Rotkin, 41; Corbis/Dewitt
Jones, 51; Corbis/Historical Picture Archive, 18; Corbis/Reuters NewMedia Inc., 31;
Corel, 16; Getty Images/Hulton Archive, 24, 37, 58; Houserstock/Dave G. Houser,
17, 44–45; Houserstock/Jan Butchofsky-Houser, 52–53; John Elk III, 48, 49;
Montana Historical Society, Helena, 26–27; Montana Historical Society, Haynes
Foundation Collection, 28; North Wind Picture Archives, 20, 29; One Mile Up Inc.,
55 (both); PhotoDisc Inc., 1; Stephen Stromstad, 21; Steve Mulligan, 10, 12–13; Tom
Till, 4, 8, 23; Travel Montana Dept. of Commerce, 56, 57; UNICORN Stock
Photos/A. Ramey, 38; UNICORN Stock Photos/Eric R. Berndt, 43; UNICORN
Stock Photos/Gary Randall, 63; UNICORN Stock Photos/Jean Higgins, 46;
UNICORN Stock Photos/Patti McConville, 32; UNICORN Stock Photos/Robert
Hitchman, 15; U.S. Postal Service, 59

Artistic Effects
Comstock, Corbis, Digital Stock, Digital Vision, PhotoDisc, Inc.

1 2 3 4 5 6 08 07 06 05 04 03

Table of Contents

On a July day, the ice melts on Iceberg Lake in Glacier National Park. Most of the year, this lake is completely frozen over.

About Montana

In Montana's Glacier National Park, towering mountain peaks reflect in clear lakes. Waterfalls spill over the mountainsides into rivers and streams.

Glacier National Park is the most visited place in Montana. Some visitors come to enjoy the peaceful quiet. Others come for adventure. Visitors can hike, ski, and bike more than 700 miles (1,130 kilometers) of trails. Some adventurers climb the famous peaks of the Rocky Mountains.

Glacier National Park is a preserve for a variety of animals. More than 70 species of mammals and 260 kinds of birds live in the park. Animals there include rare grizzly bears and wolves.

> *"Far away in northwestern Montana, hidden from view by clustering mountain peaks, lies an unmapped corner— the Crown of the Continent."*
> –George Bird Grinnell, "Father" of Glacier National Park, 1901

Glacier National Park opened in 1910. In 1932, it combined with Canada's Waterton Lakes National Park. The park became known as Waterton-Glacier International Peace Park. The park is a symbol of peace and friendship between Canada and the United States. In 1995, the park became a World Heritage site. The United Nations recognizes the park as being one of the world's most important places.

The Treasure State

Since the 1850s, people in Montana have mined for silver, gold, and copper. These riches made people call Montana the Treasure State.

Montana is the fourth-largest state. In spite of Montana's large size, less than 1 million people live there. Montana ranks 44th in population of U.S. states.

Montana is part of the Northwest. Idaho borders Montana to the south and west. Canada lies to the north of Montana. North and South Dakota border Montana to the east. Wyoming lies to Montana's south.

Montana Cities

CANADA

NORTH

DAKOTA

● Havre

● Kalispell

● Great Falls

MONTANA

● Missoula

⊛ Helena

Miles ●
City

SOUTH

DAKOTA

● Billings

Bozemzan ● ● Livingston

IDAHO

WYOMING

Scale
Miles
0   30   60   90
0   30   60   90   120
Kilometers

N
W   E
S

Legend

	American Indian Reservation
⊛	Capital
●	City

The peaks of the Continental Divide make up part of Montana's Rocky Mountains.

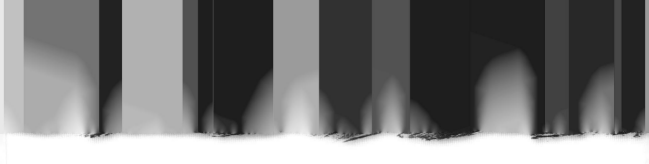

Land, Climate, and Wildlife

American Indians called Montana "the backbone of the world." This name refers to the high peaks that divide the waters of North America. This split is called the Continental Divide. West of the divide, rivers flow toward the Pacific Ocean. East of the divide, rivers flow toward the Atlantic Ocean.

Montana has two vastly different landscapes. The Rocky Mountains make up western Montana. The Great Plains covers the rest of the state.

The Rocky Mountains

Volcanic activity and slow-moving sheets of ice called glaciers created the Rocky Mountains' jagged peaks. Glaciers are still active in some of Montana's higher peaks. Snow covers the mountaintops most of the year. Low, grassy valleys lie between the mountains.

The Rocky Mountains extend from Alaska through Canada and Montana and as far south as New Mexico. More than 50 mountain ranges make up Montana's Rocky Mountains. Montana's highest point lies in the Absaroka Range. Granite Peak stands 12,799 feet (3,901 meters) above sea level.

The Great Plains

The Great Plains region in eastern Montana is grassy and bare. Mostly flat land offers an almost endless view of the horizon.

Yellow sweet clover is a type of grass that thrives on Montana's plains.

Montana's Land Features

WATERTON-GLACIER
INTERNATIONAL
PEACE PARK

Flathead
Lake

Missouri River

Fort Peck
Lake

ROCKY MOUNTAINS

GREAT PLAINS

Yellowstone River

Granite
Peak

YELLOWSTONE
NATIONAL
PARK

Scale
Miles
0   30   60   90
0   30   60   90   120
Kilometers

N
W   E
S

Legend

•••••	Continental Divide
▲	Highest Point
⬡	Lake
🏔	Mountain Range
▢	National Park
〰	River

This openness gives Montana another of its nicknames, "Big Sky Country."

The Great Plains is not entirely flat. Some areas have small mountain ranges and rolling hills. In southeastern Montana lie rocky badlands. Wind and water have sculpted rocks in this area into unusual shapes.

Rivers and Lakes

Montana is known as the headwaters state because so many rivers start in Montana. The state's largest rivers are the Missouri and the Yellowstone Rivers.

Montana's largest lakes are Flathead Lake and Fort Peck Lake. Flathead Lake is the largest natural lake in the state. Fort Peck Lake is the largest artificial lake.

Climate

Montana's climate changes with the region. In winter, the plains are cooler than the mountain areas. Montana's winters are very cold. Temperatures stay below freezing much of the time. Winter temperatures can drop below 0 degrees Fahrenheit (minus 18 degrees Celsius). In summer, western Montana tends to be cooler than the east. Montana's highest

The Missouri River winds through colorful hills and rock formations. The Missouri River is a popular recreation spot for fishing, canoeing, and kayaking.

Did you know...?
Dinosaurs once roamed
Montana. Tyrannosaurus rex,
triceratops, and other dinosaur
bones have been discovered
throughout the state. Some
scientists believe the dinosaurs
died out because of extreme
climate changes.

mountaintops can get dustings of snow in summer.

Montana's weather can change rapidly. Warm Chinook winds gust down from the eastern slopes of the mountains. These winds have raised temperatures as much as 26 degrees Fahrenheit (14 degrees Celsius) in one minute. Cold winds from the north can lower temperatures just as quickly.

Montana is a dry state. The state's annual precipitation is 15 inches (38 centimeters). The northwestern corner of Montana receives the most precipitation. The eastern half of the state is the driest. In winter, snow falls all over the state.

Plant Life

Montana's plant life also varies by region. Forests of fir, pine, cedar, birch, hemlock, and aspen trees spread across Montana's western mountains. Grasslands cover drier eastern Montana. Juniper trees, cactuses, and a few ponderosa pines also grow in eastern Montana.

Montana is famous for its wildflowers. Many types of flowers grow on Montana's mountainsides. A colorful display of wildflowers blanket Glacier National Park in summer.

Wildlife

Montana's rivers, lakes, and streams are famous fishing spots. Trout is the most common fish in Montana. Salmon, sturgeon, crappie, walleye, and perch also swim in Montana's waters.

Some of the same types of animals that lived in Montana hundreds of years ago still live there today. Grizzly bears and wolves roam some protected areas of the state. Montana is one

Wildflowers cover the grassy slopes of Logan Pass in Glacier National Park. More than 2,500 kinds of flowering plants grow in Montana.

of the last states where these animals can be found. Other large animals, such as moose, elk, deer, caribou, bighorn sheep, and mountain goats, also live mostly in Montana's mountains. Black bears find fish to eat in Montana's mountain rivers and streams.

Montana's grasslands are home to large numbers of pronghorn antelope and deer. Colonies of prairie dogs dig underground tunnels. Badgers also live in the grasslands.

Mountain goats climb the rocky ledges of Montana's mountains. Mountain goats grow a shaggy coat for winter.

Berkeley Pit

The U.S. government has named the Berkeley Pit near Butte as one of the largest toxic sites in the country. This abandoned mine pit is slowly filling with years of rainwater and melted snow. Metals in the pit poison the water. Scientists fear that the water will overflow and run into nearby rivers and towns. This could pollute the drinking water supply. People and animals could get sick from the water. Plants along the polluted rivers could die. Scientists are still undecided about how to safely clean up the pit.

One animal that is almost missing in Montana is the bison, also known as the American buffalo. Millions of bison once roamed the plains of eastern Montana.

American Indians relied on bison for food, shelter, blankets, and tools. They used almost every part of the bison.

In the late 1800s, white hunters killed almost all the bison. By 1900, less than 1,000 bison remained. Hunters killed the bison for their tongues and hides. The rest was left to rot.

Today, only a few small bison herds remain in Montana. Most herds are privately owned. Visitors can see protected bison in the National Bison Range in northwestern Montana.

The Blackfeet Indians
lived on the Great Plains
in teepees.

Chapter 3

History of Montana

Before European settlers came to Montana, American Indians lived in the area. Groups including the Blackfeet, Crow, Cheyenne, and Arapaho lived on the plains. Other groups including the Shoshone, Flathead, and Kutenai lived in the Rocky Mountains. Both the plains and mountain groups hunted bison. Before the early 1800s, almost no Europeans had been in Montana.

The Journey of Lewis and Clark

In 1803, the United States bought a large piece of land from France. The sale was called the Louisiana Purchase. Most of present-day Montana was part of the purchase.

Buffalo Jumps

Early American Indians used buffalo jumps to kill large numbers of buffalo at once. Indians would dress up in wolf skins and chase the buffalo toward a cliff. The frightened buffalo would tumble over the cliff. Some died from the fall. Others were killed by hunters waiting below.

Three known historic buffalo jump sites remain in Montana. The Ulm-Pishkin site is near Great Falls. The Madison Buffalo Jump is near Bozeman, and the Wahkpa Chu'gn is located in Havre.

President Thomas Jefferson sent Meriwether Lewis and William Clark to explore the new land. Lewis, Clark, 30 other men, and a Shoshone woman named Sacagawea arrived in Montana in 1805. In Montana, Lewis and Clark explored the Missouri and Yellowstone Rivers. On the way back from the West Coast, Clark found a large rock formation. Clark carved his name into it on July 25, 1806, and named it Pompey's Pillar. Clark's etching is the only visible proof that remains of the journey. Today, visitors can follow the explorers' journey on the Lewis and Clark historic trail.

William Clark carved his name and the date into the sandstone of Pompey's Pillar.

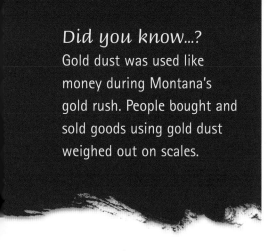

Early Settlers

Lewis and Clark reported that many beaver and otter lived in the Montana area. In the early 1800s, fur traders came to Montana. They built trading posts like Fort Henry and Fort Benton.

Missionaries also came to Montana. They built churches and missions, hoping to convert the American Indians to Christianity.

The Gold Rush

In the late 1850s and early 1860s, gold was found in Montana. Many miners came to the state. Bannack, Virginia City, and other mining towns seemed to be built overnight. Last Chance Gulch was another place where gold was found. This town later became Montana's capital, Helena.

Mining towns were wild and dangerous. Most towns did not have elected lawmen or town officers. Robbery and murder were common. People began to take the law into their own hands. In Virginia City, locals discovered that the town sheriff was an outlaw leader. He and 21 of his gang members were hanged by people trying to restore order.

Ghost Towns

After gold ran out in some areas, miners quickly moved on to new gold strikes. Towns were abandoned as quickly as they were put up. Abandoned mining towns are called ghost towns. Montana has more than 50 ghost towns. Bannack State Park (at left) near Dillon preserves the remains of Montana's first gold strikes. Visitors can tour the jailhouse, hotel, and sheriff's quarters.

Settlement

Other people came to Montana to settle the fertile land. In 1862, the Homestead Act was passed to encourage people to settle the west. The U.S. government gave land to settlers for farming or cattle grazing.

Montana was a part of Idaho Territory until 1864. That year, the U.S. government made Montana a separate territory. Federal officers went to the territory to restore order. Montana became a safer place for miners and settlers.

General Custer (middle) and his troops were defeated in Montana's Little Big Horn Valley.

American Indian Conflicts

As more settlers came to Montana and other western territories, conflicts with American Indians increased. New settlers often took American Indians' land. Two of the most famous U.S. battles with American Indians took place in Montana.

In 1876, the U.S. Calvary followed several American Indian groups into Montana's Little Big Horn Valley. General George

"I am tired of fighting . . . from where the sun now stands, I will fight no more."

–Chief Joseph, leader of the Nez Percé Indians, 1877

Custer planned a surprise attack on the American Indians. The 600 men split up into three groups of about 200 men each. The Sioux, Cheyenne, and Arapaho Indians were waiting for Custer and his group. Thousands of American Indians overwhelmed Custer and his men, killing all of them. This battle is known as the Battle of Little Bighorn, or as Custer's Last Stand.

In 1877, the Nez Percé Indians were also chased by the U.S. Calvary. About 800 Nez Percé were forced from their homeland in Oregon. They fled through Idaho, Wyoming, and Montana hoping to find safety in Canada. The U.S. Calvary trapped them in Montana about 40 miles (64 kilometers) from the Canadian border. Nez Percé leader Chief Joseph surrendered. His people were starving and freezing to death. The Nez Percé were forced onto a reservation in Indian Territory, or present-day Oklahoma.

The U.S. government and settlers wanted land across the whole continent. The government forced American Indians from Montana and all across the nation onto reservations.

Growing Industry and Statehood

Cattle ranching and mining became major industries in the 1870s and 1880s. Ranchers brought thousands of cattle into the state. Montana's mining industry grew to include silver, copper, and coal.

Life in Montana was not easy for ranchers and miners. Drought and severe winters killed many cattle. Some miners became rich, but most did not. Miners worked long hours. The job was often dangerous. In the 1870s, miners formed unions to fight for better working conditions and more pay.

William A. Clark and Marcus Daly each became rich from selling copper. They were known as Montana's "Copper Kings." Clark and Daly were business rivals. Both men wanted different cities to be the state capital. Anaconda was Daly's company town, so he wanted the capital there. Clark had many business investments in Helena and wanted it to be the capital. Both men spent millions of dollars trying to persuade the government. Clark won, and Helena became Montana's capital.

New industries and the building of railroads brought many people into the state. More than 100,000 people moved to

Miners used water flumes to separate gold from the rocks in Confederate Gulch. Confederate Gulch was a mining district in Montana's Big Belt Mountains.

Montana between 1880 and 1890. Some of the newcomers were Chinese immigrants. Many of them mined or helped build railroads. The Chinese were treated poorly in Montana. Many Chinese left Montana once the railroads were built and the mining boom was over.

In 1889, Montana finally had enough people to become a state. On November 8, 1889, Montana became the 41st state to enter the Union. Joseph K. Toole became the state's first governor.

A section gang made up of Chinese immigrants works along a stretch of Montana's railroads.

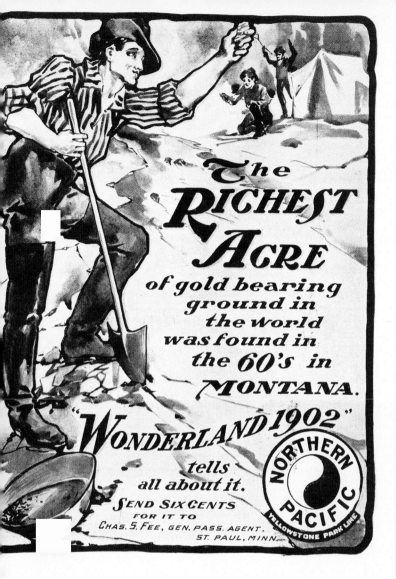

Railroad companies used advertisements to attract settlers to Montana.

The Early 1900s and the Great Depression

In the early 1900s, railroad owners tried to attract people to Montana. They advertised the state as a place with rich farmland and great beauty. Settlers moved to Montana with high expectations.

Some people were able to make a living in Montana, and some people were not. Periods of drought made farming difficult. When their crops failed, farmers were forced to give up their land.

The Great Depression (1929–1939) also caused hardship for farmers and other workers. The demand for products decreased. Many people lost their jobs and land.

Montana's economy recovered with federal programs and the start of World War II (1939–1945). The building of the Fort Peck Dam and other projects created jobs for Montanans. Demand for Montana's products increased during the war, creating more jobs.

Recent Years

Many changes took place in Montana's economy in the mid-1900s. After World War II, the state's economy relied less on agriculture. Industries such as oil and coal mining became more important. More people moved from rural areas to towns and cities to find jobs.

In the 1960s and 1970s, Montana tried to use its natural resources more efficiently and environmentally. Several hydroelectric dams were built to use the energy created by running water. Environmental restrictions were placed on mining companies to protect Montana's land, air, and soil.

In the 1980s and 1990s, several small radical groups formed in Montana. These groups were against the government. Some refused

Police lead Unabomber Theodore Kaczynski away from the Helena Federal Courthouse. Kaczynski mailed packages with bombs that exploded when people opened them.

to pay taxes or obey laws. Individuals or groups sometimes threatened or endangered people. Theodore Kaczynski, who became known as the Unabomber, mailed packages with bombs in them. The bombs killed three people and injured several others. In 1996, Kaczynski was captured near Lincoln.

The statue of a man on horseback was added to Montana's capitol building in 1905. This statue honors General Thomas Francis Meagher from Montana Territory, who fought in the Civil War.

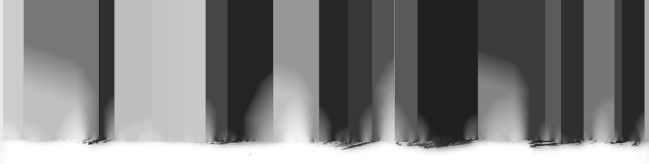

Government and Politics

In 1969, Montanans decided that their first constitution was outdated. They called for a convention to write a new constitution. Montana's legislature wrote and approved the new constitution in 1972.

Montana's new constitution is thought to be one of the most progressive in the country. Montana's citizens have more rights than most state citizens have. For example, Montana's constitution promises the right to a clean, healthy environment.

Branches of Government

Montana's constitution divides the government into three branches. These branches are the executive, legislative, and judicial branches.

The executive branch carries out laws. The governor heads the executive branch. The governor signs bills into law and appoints some officials. He or she has the power to reject, or veto, certain items of a bill and pass the rest of it. Six other officials make up the executive branch. All six of these officials answer to the governor. All officials in the executive branch are elected to 4-year terms. They may serve no more than two terms in a row.

Montana's legislative branch suggests and passes laws. The legislature is divided into the house of representatives and the senate. The 100 representatives are elected to 2-year terms. They cannot serve more than four terms. The 50 members of the senate are elected to 4-year terms. They cannot serve more than two terms. The legislature can pass a law vetoed by the governor if enough members agree.

Montana's judicial branch interprets laws and tries court cases. Montana's supreme court is the highest court. It can overrule decisions made by lower courts. The supreme court has one chief justice and six associate justices. Each justice is

Montana's State Government

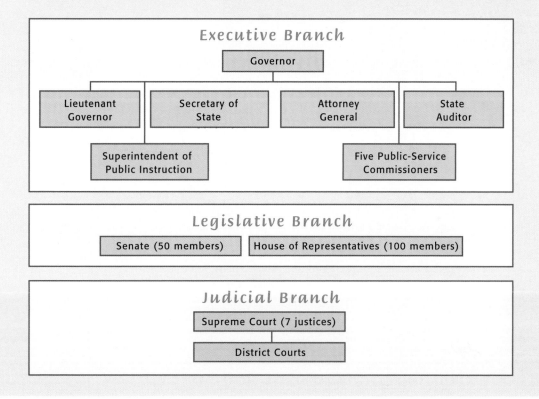

Executive Branch

Governor

Lieutenant Governor

Secretary of State

Attorney General

State Auditor

Superintendent of Public Instruction

Five Public-Service Commissioners

Legislative Branch

Senate (50 members)

House of Representatives (100 members)

Judicial Branch

Supreme Court (7 justices)

District Courts

elected to an 8-year term. Major civil and criminal cases are tried in district courts. Judges in Montana's district courts serve 6-year terms. Municipal courts, justice of the peace courts, and other special courts hear less serious civil and criminal cases.

> *"In every true Montanan there is something that says, 'I am a last holdout.'"*
>
> —David Lamb, author of *A Sense of Place: Listening to Americans*

Local Government

Montana's local governments take care of the daily needs of communities. Most of the state's 56 counties elect three county commissioners to govern the counties. Many of Montana's cities and towns use the mayor-council form of government. Other cities and towns use a council-manager system.

National Government and Politics

Montana also participates in national government. Like all U.S. states, Montana sends two senators to the U.S. Senate. Because of its small population, Montana sends only one representative to the U.S. House of Representatives.

Montana's voters used to favor the Democratic Party, but that is changing. Since the 1960s, an increasing number of Republican candidates have been elected in Montana. Montana has voted for only one Democratic presidential candidate since 1968.

Jeanette Rankin

In 1916, Jeanette Rankin, from Missoula, became the first woman to be elected to the U.S. Congress. Rankin represented Montana in the U.S. House of Representatives.

Rankin helped fight for an amendment that would give women the right to vote. This amendment, called women's suffrage, became law in 1920.

Rankin also fought against war. In 1918, she lost her seat in the House. She was not reelected because she had voted against war on Germany in World War I. In 1940, Rankin was again elected to the U.S. House of Representatives. She was the only one to vote against going to war with Japan. She said that because as a woman she could not go to war, she refused to send anyone else. After Rankin left office, she continued to protest war until she died in 1973. The Jeanette Rankin Peace Center in Missoula was founded to uphold Rankin's nonviolent beliefs.

Park rangers at Logan Pass educate a visitor about Glacier National Park.

Chapter 5

Economy and Resources

Montana's economy has changed with the times. Mining and agriculture used to be the state's major industries. Montana's economy still depends on its natural resources, but recently, service industries have become more important. Tourism is now a major industry in Montana.

Wages in Montana are lower than the national average. The government is working to bring better-paying jobs to the state.

Service Industries

Many Montanans work in service industries. These industries account for most of the state's income. Service industries

include health care, education, tourism, retail stores, government, real estate, and finance.

Tourism is becoming an important service industry in the state. Tourists spend more than $2 billion a year in Montana. Montanans in the tourism industry work as ski-lift operators, raft and fishing guides, and hotel and restaurant workers.

The government employs nearly 20 percent of Montanans. Many Montanans working in tourism are employed by the government. Some of these people work at Montana's state and national parks.

Mining

Montana is rich in natural resources. Coal and petroleum are the state's leading mining products. Most of the state's coal and petroleum mining takes place in eastern Montana.

Metals such as gold, silver, copper, and lead are still mined in Montana. Gold is Montana's most valuable mined metal. Most metal mining takes place in Montana's southern Rocky Mountains.

In recent years, mining in Montana has declined for several reasons. Much of the decline is because metal and mineral resources have been nearly used up. Companies often do not find enough quality resources to make mining profitable. Also, years of unrestricted mining have caused damage to the land and water supply. In recent years, the state government has made mining companies responsible

Miners in protective suits look for metals in an underground mine. The lights on their helmets help them find their way in the dark.

"The big challenge for Montanans is to reach a balance on issues. I believe when it comes to managing resources such as coal, timber, or natural gas, both sides can have their needs met. We can develop jobs, energy, and resources, while also being concerned for the environment."
—Mike Foster, Chief Policy Advisor to
Montana's Office of the Governor

for damage they have caused. The government and mining companies must also research the possible effects of mining on the environment. This study often takes time. Mining companies are not always willing to wait. The companies may decide to mine in countries with fewer restrictions.

Montanans have different opinions about these new laws. Some people think that jobs for Montanans are more important than the environment. Others think Montana's most valuable industry is tourism. They want to keep the environment clean so tourists come to the state. The government is trying to manage both sides. It is always looking for new ways to mine without hurting the environment.

Manufacturing

Most of Montana's manufactured products are made from raw materials mined, harvested, or raised in the state. Petroleum

A large saw blade cuts through a tree log before the bark is removed. Logs are sent to manufacturers in Montana who make lumber and paper products from the wood.

refining is Montana's leading manufacturing business. Other manufacturers make lumber and wood products from Montana's trees. Machinery and food processing are also important.

Agriculture, Ranching, and Timber

Farming and ranching are major industries in eastern Montana. Farms cover about two-thirds of Montana's total land. Most of this land is used for grazing livestock. The rest is used for raising crops.

Livestock accounts for half of Montana's agricultural income. Beef from cattle is Montana's leading agricultural product. Bison are also raised for meat. Bison meat is becoming popular because it has less fat than beef. Sheep and hogs are also raised in the state.

Wheat is the state's largest crop. Montana ranks third in wheat production. Barley, sugar beets, hay, potatoes, and sweet cherries are also grown in Montana.

The timber industry is also important to western Montana. Fir, pine, spruce, and cedar trees are some of the trees harvested in Montana. These trees are used for lumber, furniture, and other wood products. Montana is also a major producer of Christmas trees.

Cattle graze on a pasture in Stevensville. Montana has about 2.7 million cattle, which is almost three times as many cattle as people.

A bucking horse tries to throw his rider off at a rodeo in Dillon. Many Montanans enjoy watching or participating in rodeos.

Chapter 6

People and Culture

Montana is a state of small cities surrounded by vast rural areas. Many people have settled in Montana to enjoy nature and the wide-open spaces. They have also come to avoid the pressures of big city life. Montana has been called the "Last Best Place."

Western Heritage

Montana's western heritage is celebrated in many ways. Visitors and residents enjoy watching and participating in rodeos. In rodeos, cowboys compete in horseback riding and calf-roping events. One of the most famous rodeos is the Wild Horse Stampede in Wolf Point.

Visitors who want to experience traditional western living go to Montana's ranches. There, they can participate in cattle round-ups, cattle branding, and chuck wagon feasts.

In June, a reenactment of the Battle of Little Bighorn is performed. Men dressed as soldiers and American Indians recreate the battle to educate visitors. People can also visit a museum on the grounds.

To celebrate Montana's first explorers, the state devotes several celebrations to Lewis and Clark. Clark Day is celebrated at Pompey's Pillar near Billings. Visitors can listen to music and eat buffalo burgers on the land that Lewis and Clark explored.

American Indians compete in a powwow during North American Indian Days. This celebration is held on the Blackfeet Reservation in Browning.

Charles Russell

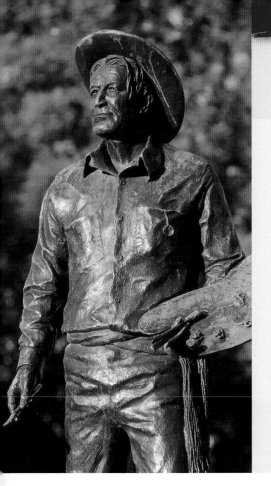

Charles Russell came to Montana at age 16 to be a cowboy. Russell had no formal art training, but he drew wherever he went. He was nicknamed "Kid" Russell and the "Cowboy Artist." Many of Russell's drawings and paintings portray American Indian life.

Charles Russell is considered one of the greatest western artists. The Montana Historical Society Museum in Helena displays some of his art. The C. M. Russell Museum in Great Falls is dedicated to Russell's life and works of art. A statue of Russell (at left) is located there.

The Lewis and Clark Festival in Great Falls includes reenactments, classes, crafts, and authentic frontier food cooked over a campfire.

American Indians also celebrate their heritage. Many annual powwows and fairs take place. In July, the Blackfeet celebrate North American Indian Days in Browning on the Blackfeet Reservation. The Crow have a famous powwow on their reservation in August. The powwow includes a fair and an all-Indian rodeo.

Montana's Ethnic Background

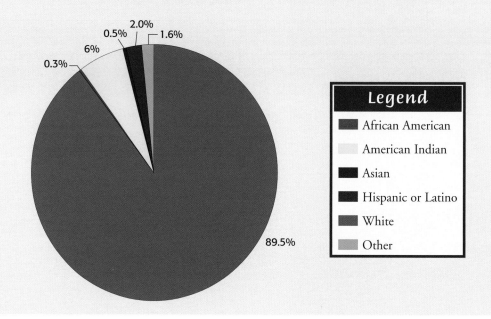

0.3%
6%
0.5%
2.0%
1.6%
89.5%

Legend
- African American
- American Indian
- Asian
- Hispanic or Latino
- White
- Other

Montana's Ethnic Backgrounds

Almost 90 percent of Montanans are white with European backgrounds. Many of them moved to Montana from the eastern United States. Others immigrated from England, Germany, Ireland, Poland, and Italy.

At 6 percent of the state's population, American Indians are Montana's second largest ethnic group. Many American Indian groups live in the state. These groups are Blackfeet, Assiniboine, Gros Ventre, Crow, Cheyenne, Sioux, Salish, Kootenai, and

Chippewa-Cree. Some of these groups live on one of Montana's seven reservations. Montana's largest reservation is the Blackfeet Reservation near Glacier National Park.

Montana is also home to about 40 small communities of religious people called Hutterites. The Hutterites came to Montana from Germany in the early 1900s. They speak German and English. The Hutterites own large farms and ranches. They share goods and property within their communities. Hutterites do not own TVs, radios, or guns. They do not use modern appliances. They do not believe in fighting wars. Hutterites try to keep their traditional way of life unchanged.

Hutterite women usually wear colorful dresses, black and white scarves over their hair, and plaid aprons.

Sports and Recreation

Montanans love to watch and participate in sports. The state does not have any professional teams, but Montanans support their college sports teams in Missoula, Billings, Butte, and Bozeman. Several minor league baseball teams play in Montana. Montanans also hold an annual dogsled race called the Race to the Sky.

Montanans enjoy the outdoors. The wide-open space gives Montanans plenty of room for recreation. Montanans enjoy fishing and boating in Montana's lakes and rivers. They mountain climb, ski, hike, ride horses, hunt, and camp in the mountains.

Perceptions

It seems that Hollywood also appreciates Montana's beauty. Many movies have showcased the state's landscape. Some of these movies include *The Horse Whisperer*, *The River Wild*, *Far and Away*, and *A River Runs Through It*.

Montana is a large state with a small population. Montanans are known to be independent. They like to be thought of as individuals, with individual opinions and beliefs. Montanans value nature and their vast landscapes as places to work, relax, and call home.

Fishing is a popular sport in Montana. Visitors and residents fish for trout in Montana's rivers and streams.

Recipe: Black Cherry Pie

Montana's main fruit crop is cherries, which are grown mostly around Flathead Lake. In 1989, hundreds of cherry trees were destroyed by a frost. Cherry farmers are still recovering. Use fresh, frozen, or canned black cherries to make a pie.

Ingredients

2 cups (480 mL) black cherries, pitted
1 cup (240 mL) sugar
3 tablespoons (45 mL) cornstarch
½ cup (120 mL) water
4 teaspoons (20 mL) lemon juice
1 9-inch (23-centimeter) premade graham cracker pie crust in an aluminum tin
4 cups (960 mL) black cherries, pitted
8 ounces (220 mL) whipped topping

Equipment

medium saucepan
fork or potato masher
dry ingredient
    measuring cups
measuring spoons
liquid ingredient
    measuring cup

What You Do

1. In the saucepan, mash 2 cups (480 mL) of the cherries with a fork or potato masher.

2. Add sugar to the cherries and mix together.

3. Stir in cornstarch, and then stir in the water.

4. Cook cherry mixture at medium heat, stirring until the mixture is thick and transparent.

5. Remove from the heat.

6. Add lemon juice to the mixture.

7. Place the 4 cups (960 mL) of uncooked cherries into the crust.

8. Pour cooked cherry mixture over the cherries in the crust.

9. Chill at least 4 hours before serving.

10. Spread whipped topping over the pie.

Makes 6 servings

Montana's Flag and Seal

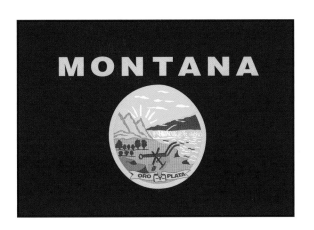

Montana's Flag

Montana's state flag shows the state seal on a blue background. The state's name is printed in gold above the seal. The flag was adopted in 1905.

Montana's State Seal

Montana's seal shows the state's history and natural beauty. In the background, the sun rises above the mountains, a waterfall, and the Missouri River. In the foreground, a pick and shovel stand for Montana's mining industry. The plow stands for agriculture. A banner with the state motto, "Oro y Plata," meaning "Gold and Silver," lies below the tools. Around the seal are the words, "The Great Seal of the State of Montana." The seal was adopted in 1965 and has been changed several times.

Almanac

General Facts

Nicknames: Treasure State, Big Sky Country

Population: 902,195 (U.S. Census 2000)
Population rank: 44th

Capital: Helena

Largest cities: Billings, Missoula, Great Falls, Butte, Bozeman

Agricultural products: Livestock, wheat, cherries, sugar beets, hay, barley, potatoes

Agriculture

Average winter temperature: 20 degrees Fahrenheit (minus 7 degrees Celsius)

Average summer temperature: 64 degrees Fahrenheit (18 degrees Celsius)

Average annual precipitation: 15 inches (38 centimeters)

Climate

Area: 147,046 square miles (380,849 square kilometers)
Size rank: 4th

Highest point: Granite Peak, 12,799 feet (3,901 meters) above sea level

Lowest point: Kootenai River, 1,800 feet (549 meters) above sea level

Geography

Western meadowlark

Bitterroot

Animal: Grizzly bear

Bird: Western meadowlark

Fish: Blackspotted cutthroat trout

Flower: Bitterroot

Fossil: Maiasaura

Economy

Natural resources: Petroleum, coal, gold, silver, copper, timber

Types of industry: Service, mining, agriculture, manufacturing

Symbols

Grass: Bluebunch wheatgrass

Motto: "Oro y Plata," which means "Gold and Silver" in Spanish

Song: "Montana," written by Charles Cohan, composed by Joseph E. Howard

Tree: Ponderosa pine

Government

First governor: Joseph K. Toole, 1889–1893 and 1901–1908

Statehood: November 8, 1889; 41st state

U.S. Representative: 1

U.S. Senators: 2

U.S. electoral votes: 3

Counties: 56

Timeline

State History

1805–1806
Lewis and Clark explore Montana.

1877
The Nez Percé Indians surrender in Montana.

1876
American Indians kill General Custer and his men in the Battle of Little Bighorn.

1864
Montana becomes a separate territory.

U.S. History

1775–1783
Colonists fight for independence from the British in the Revolutionary War.

1861–1865
The North and the South fight the Civil War.

1620
Pilgrims settle in North America.

1916

Jeanette Rankin from Montana becomes the first woman elected to the U.S. Congress.

1910

Glacier National Park opens.

1996

Theodore Kaczynksi, the Unabomber, is captured near Lincoln.

1889

Montana becomes the 41st state on November 8.

1972

Montana's new state constitution is adopted.

1914–1918

World War I is fought; the United States enters the war in 1917.

1964

The Civil Rights Act is passed, making discrimination illegal.

1929–1939

The United States experiences economic hardship in the Great Depression.

1939–1945

World War II is fought; the United States enters the war in 1941.

2001

Terrorists attack the World Trade Center and the Pentagon on September 11.

Words to Know

badlands (BAD-landz)—areas where wind and water have sculpted rocks into unusual formations

bison (BYE-suhn)—a large animal with a big shaggy head, broad shoulders, and horns; the bison is also known as the American buffalo.

Continental Divide (kon-tun-EHN-tuhl duh-VIDE)—the high peaks of the Rocky Mountains that divide river waters; rivers west of the divide flow toward the Pacific Ocean, and rivers east of the divide flow toward the Atlantic Ocean.

glacier (GLAY-shur)—a large sheet of slow-moving ice

Hutterites (HUH-tuh-rites)—a religious group of people from Germany who live without modern appliances and do not believe in war

powwow (POW-wow)—a traditional American Indian celebration

precipitation (pri-sip-i-TAY-shuhn)—water that falls from the sky in the form of rain, snow, sleet, or hail

radical (RAD-i-kuhl)—extreme; radical groups in Montana have extreme political views.

toxic (TOK-sik)—poisonous; the Berkeley Pit is a toxic site.

To Learn More

Gibson, Karen Bush. *The Blackfeet: People of the Dark Moccasins.* American Indian Nations. Mankato, Minn.: Bridgestone Books, 2003.

Hirschmann, Kris. *Montana: The Treasure State.* World Almanac Library of the States. Milwaukee: World Almanac Library, 2003.

LaDoux, Rita C. *Montana.* Hello U.S.A. Minneapolis: Lerner Publications, 2003.

Williams, Judith M. *Montana.* From Sea to Shining Sea. New York: Children's Press, 2002.

Internet Sites

Do you want to find out more about Montana?
Let FactHound, our fact-finding hound dog, do the research for you.

Here's how:
1) Visit *http://www.facthound.com*
2) Type in the **Book ID** number:
   0736821848
3) Click on **FETCH IT.**

FactHound will fetch Internet sites picked by our editors just for you!

Places to Write and Visit

Glacier National Park
P.O. Box 128
West Glacier, MT 59936

Governor's Office
State Capitol
Helena, MT 59620-0801

Little Bighorn Battlefield National Monument
P.O. Box 39
Exit 510 Off I-90 Highway 212
Crow Agency, MT 59022-0039

Montana Historical Society
P.O. Box 201201
225 North Roberts
Helena, MT 59620-1201

Travel Montana
P.O. Box 200533
Helena, MT 59620-0533

Index

Mount Gould towers over Josephine Lake in Glacier National Park.